# Discover the
# Vikings

## Everyday Life, Art and Culture

## John C. Miles

W

Franklin Watts

First published in Great Britain in 2016 by The Watts Publishing Group

Credits
Series Editor: Amy Stephenson
Series Designer: Jane Hawkins
Picture researcher: Diana Morris

Picture credits: Amitai/Dreamstime: 16c. Anielius/Shutterstock: front cover t. David Hjort Blindell/ Dreamstime: 25t. The British Museum: front cover main. De Agostini/Superstock: 1b, 24b. Dave Donaldson/ Alamy: 27b. Donatas1205/Shutterstock: front cover b, 1t. Elena Duvernay/Dreamstime: 9b. Muhammed Junaedi Firmansyah/Dreamstime: 5bl. Glen Harper/Alamy: 29t. Heritage/Superstock: 29b. Holmes Garden Photos/Alamy: 22b. Cindy Hopkins/Alamy: 12b. Illiiioiiilll/Shutterstock: front cover bg. Ying Feng Johansson/ Dreamstime: 26c. Jorvik Centre, York: 18c. JPS/Shutterstock: 10b. Lennart Larsen. CC-BY-SA National Museum, Denmark. http://samlinger.natmus.dk/DO/2094: 4t, 5br, 6t, 6c, 8t, 9c, 10t, 11b, 12t, 14t, 15b, 16t, 18t, 19c, 20t, 21br, 22t, 22c, 24t, 25bl, 26t, 27tl, 28t. Michael Melford/Getty Images: 14b. National Library of Iceland. Kalfalaekjarbok: 27tr. National Museum Denmark. CC-BT-SA: 25br. Alexander Ozerov/Dreamstime: 4c. Jamen Percy/Dreamstime: 17b. Photononstop/Superstock: 15t. Private Collection/BAL: 23b. Olivier Le Queinec/Shutterstock: front cover bg. © Ribe Viking Centre: 11t. © Rosala Viking Centre 2016: 20c. Skyscan Photolibrary/Alamy: 6b. Jean Soutif/Look at Sciences/SPL: 8c. Doug Steley/Alamy: 13t. Szvivi/Dreamstime: 13b. Thjodminjasfn Reykjavik/Werner Forman Archive: 21bl. wikimedia commons/Parker Library, Cambridge: 28b. Anna Yakimova/Dreamstime: 7t. York Archaeological Trust: 19bl, 19br.

HB ISBN: 978 1 4451 4887 8

PB ISBN: 978 1 4451 5370 4

Printed in China

Franklin Watts
An imprint of
Hachette Children's Group
Part of The Watts Publishing Group
Carmelite House
50 Victoria Embankment
London EC4Y 0DZ


An Hachette UK Company
www.hachette.co.uk


www.franklinwatts.co.uk

# Contents

# Who were the Vikings?

The Vikings were people who lived in the Scandinavian lands of Norway, Sweden and Denmark around 1,200 years ago. Some Vikings left their homelands and went raiding and exploring in other parts of Europe and the wider world.

▲ In much of Scandinavia, farming land is found in small patches next to the sea or along sea inlets, called fjords.

## Viking homelands

In Norway and parts of Sweden the land is mountainous, rocky and covered with forests. In Denmark the land is flatter, but the soil can be poor. The climate in Scandinavian countries is extreme, with long, cold, dark winters.

## Warriors

In the late CE 700s, groups of Viking warriors set off to go raiding - looking for valuables to steal. This brought them into contact with other parts of Europe and Asia. Because of their raiding, Vikings had a reputation for being bloodthirsty pirates.

## Jarls rule

The most powerful jarls commanded hundreds of warriors. Over time, they defeated other jarls and took their land until, late in the Viking Age, one king ruled each Scandinavian country.

## Merchants and traders

Not all Vikings were warriors. Some were farmers and some were merchants who made long voyages to sell the produce of their homelands. Others were craft workers who made beautiful objects out of metals, such as gold, silver and bronze. Viking woodworkers carved timber with beautiful, intricate patterns. Viking shipbuilders made vessels that could survive long ocean voyages.

▼ The Viking homelands were the modern-day Scandinavian countries of Norway, Sweden and Denmark.

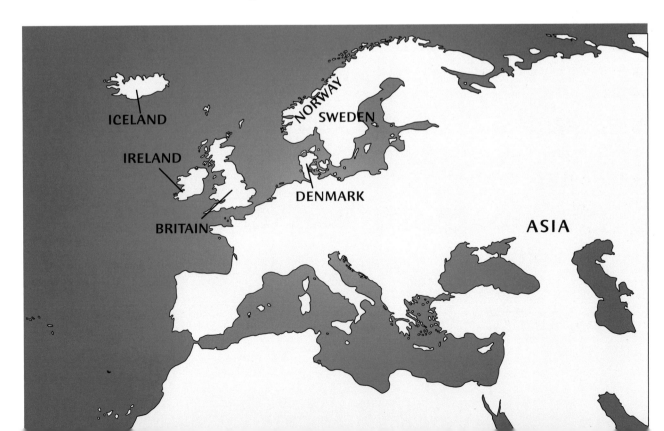

ICELAND

IRELAND

BRITAIN

NORWAY

SWEDEN

DENMARK

ASIA

# Raiders from the sea

Beginning in the late 700s, groups of fierce Viking warriors spread terror throughout many parts of Christian Europe. People prayed to God to deliver them 'from the wrath of the Northmen'.

## Landing and looting

Arriving by sea, Vikings attacked local people and stole jewellery, money and other valuables. They also kidnapped locals and sold them as slaves back home. This raiding activity could make Vikings very wealthy.

Churches and monasteries, such as Lindisfarne in north-east England, were especially at risk from Viking raids because they contained gold and silver treasure and were poorly defended. ▼

### APPROACHING TERROR

If you had lived near a European coastline in the 800s, you might have seen Viking ships approaching. Your choice would have been to flee or fight. Running away would probably have been the best idea, so you would have helped gather up as many possessions as you could before the Viking raiders landed.

▲ Modern re-enactors dressed as Viking raiders carry swords, axes and shields.

## Money hungry

The first Viking raiders snatched valuables and then went back to their homelands. Later groups of Vikings stayed put until they were paid money to leave.

## Why did Vikings emigrate?

When the population in Scandinavia began to expand, overcrowding and lack of good farmland meant that people couldn't grow enough food, so some Vikings set off to live permanently in lands they had

### WHAT DID VIKING WARRIORS LOOK LIKE?

Viking warriors were well armed, with sharp swords and other weapons such as axes or spears. They carried decorated round shields made of wood and wore cone-shaped helmets. Wealthy chieftains wore chain mail – armour made from hundreds of interlocking iron rings – to protect them in battle.

once raided. Other Vikings made long sea voyages to find uninhabited places in which to start new lives. Today we might call these Vikings 'economic migrants'.

# Ships and the sea

Vikings were expert sailors, and ships and the sea were at the heart of everyday life. Scandinavian shipbuilders crafted beautiful and practical vessels for warfare and raiding as well as carrying cargo over long distances.

▲This picture shows skilled Viking shipwrights building a longship. The artist has cut away part of the ship's hull to show its wooden ribs.

## Practical design

Longships were pointed at both the bow (front) and the stern (back). This meant that they could be rowed in reverse easily - handy for a quick getaway. Longship hulls were shallow, and could be navigated in only one metre of water, allowing Viking raiding parties to make landings on beaches or sail up shallow rivers to plunder settlements.

## Building a ship

To build a longship, Vikings first constructed the keel, the long piece of wood that acted as the backbone of the vessel. Then they raised the hull (body) of the ship using overlapping long planks and crossways ribs. Early in Viking times hull planks were split from huge trees, which meant that they were much stronger than boards that had been cut with saws. Shipbuilders

preferred oak wood because it is very strong. It also gets harder with exposure to weather.

## Other vessels

Viking seafarers used smaller vessels, too. The *karve* was a small longship that was used for both warfare and carrying cargo. It had a somewhat broader hull than the larger types. The *knorr* carried cargo, such as wool, timber, wheat and livestock. They may also have been used to transport Viking settlers to faraway colonies.

### NAVIGATION

Vikings knew all about winds, tides and currents, so they were well able to find their way at sea. Nevertheless there are stories of Vikings losing their way – this was known as *hafvilla*, or 'bewildered'. Lost Viking sailors sometimes followed birds, as their flight could lead to landfall.

Viking longships were long, narrow and light for their size. They were rigged with a large square cloth sail on a short mast to catch the wind; rowers propelled the ship when the wind dropped. ▼

# Vikings at home

Viking families lived in longhouses - rectangular one-roomed buildings in which everyone worked, ate, played and slept. Longhouses were cool in summer and cosy in winter.

## Local materials

In places with many trees, Vikings built longhouses from wood. Roofs made of thatch (bundled straw) kept out the rain. In areas with harsh climates and few trees, stone houses with turf roofs were common.

A modern reconstruction of a wooden Viking longhouse. ▼

## Life inside

Inside a longhouse, the walls were lined with wooden panelling. Window openings were rare because they let rain and cold in. A fire for heating and cooking blazed on a central stone hearth. People sat on benches to eat and slept on raised

▲ Re-enactors inside a Viking longhouse. Not all longhouses had windows.

platforms along the sides of the longhouse. Animal furs or quilts kept them warm in winter.

## Bath time

Vikings bathed once a week in the bathhouse or sauna. This was a communal building where stones were heated on a fire; water was then thrown over the stones to make steam. The steam made people sweat, which washed the dirt off their skin. Vikings were clean people who liked to keep their hair tidy. Archaeologists digging up Viking sites have unearthed many combs, usually made from wood or animal bone.

### IF YOU WERE A VIKING…

Longhouses had no inside toilets, you would have had to go outside and use a hole in the ground with a wooden seat over it. You would have used sheep's wool or leaves as toilet paper.

### BOYS AND GIRLS

Viking children didn't go to school. If you were a Viking boy you would have spent time learning to fight and farm, or learn a craft such as shipbuilding. Viking girls learned how to cook, spin wool to make cloth and run a home. Like children around the world both boys and girls made time for play and games.

# Dress like a Viking

The clothing that Vikings wore was practical, but sometimes had beautiful features, such as decorated edges. The main focus was on warmth, as most Vikings lived in northern Europe, with its cool summers and freezing winters.

## Tunics and trousers

Viking men wore a long woollen tunic. This went over trousers made of wool or leather, or woollen hose (thick stockings). A belt worn over the tunic was useful for carrying a knife or other tools, and sturdy leather shoes or boots completed a Viking man's outfit.

## Women's clothing

Women wore an ankle-length woollen dress, with a shorter over-dress on top. The over-dress had open sides and was fastened at the shoulders with pins, some of which were made from silver or other precious metals. Some women would have worn a thin belt called a girdle, which

◄ Viking men and women held their cloaks together with highly decorated clasps and pins.

◀ These re-enactors show how Viking men and women typically dressed.

## Making clothing

Clothing was made at home by Viking women and girls. Wool from the family's sheep was collected, spun into yarn and woven into cloth. Dyes extracted from plants were used to colour the cloth brown, red, yellow or blue. Dyed cloth could then be cut and sewn into clothing.

▼ Viking sheep breeds, like this modern soay sheep, were smaller and easily able to withstand harsh conditions.

was handy for carrying tools, a purse or other everyday objects. In winter, everyone wore cloaks, hats and animal furs to keep warm. Viking children were dressed in smaller versions of what their parents wore.

### WHAT'S UNDERNEATH?

Both sexes wore woollen underwear. This not only kept Vikings warm, but also meant that outer garments needed washing less often as they didn't touch the skin and get soaked with sweat.

# Viking food

There were no supermarkets, so Vikings had to produce all their own food. Viking farmers in Scandinavia and the far north of Britain farmed in a challenging climate, with long, cold winters and short summers.

## Crops and animals

Viking farmers grew wheat and rye to make bread, oats to make porridge and barley to brew beer. They raised sheep, pigs and cattle. Animals provided both meat, and hides to make into leather. Vikings also grew vegetables, such as cabbages, onions and peas.

## Wild stuff

To add to their diet, Vikings hunted deer, seals, rabbits and other game animals, and caught fish from the sea or in rivers. In some areas, seabirds were an important source of food.

This photograph shows small cakes cooking on an iron griddle. ▼

### IF YOU WERE A VIKING...

You might have helped your family cook meals over the fire on the central hearth of your longhouse. Often food was stewed in a cauldron hanging over the flames. Small griddle cakes would be cooked on a piece of iron. You would have eaten from wooden dishes using a spoon and a knife or your fingers. There were no forks.

▲ The remains of the Jarlshof site in Shetland contains remains from many historical peoples, not just the Vikings.

## Preserving food

There were no refrigerators in Viking times, so Vikings pickled fish and meat in saltwater and packed it into jars or barrels to be eaten during the winter. Food could also be air-dried on wooden racks or smoked over a fire to keep it from going off.

### UNCOVERING THE EVIDENCE

On the southern tip of the Shetland Islands in Scotland, experts found a Viking farming settlement with the remains of seven Viking houses. These were built with stone walls and had roofs of wood covered with turf. There are also buildings for animals to shelter in during the winter, a forge to make iron tools and a sauna.

# Exploration and trade

Not all Viking voyages were about raiding. Merchants journeyed far and wide selling the produce of the Viking lands. Settlers crossed vast stretches of hostile ocean to find places in which to start new lives.

▲ Constantinople, now Istanbul, was a wealthy trading centre in Viking times.

## Viking merchants

Viking merchants crossed the Baltic Sea and voyaged up rivers, such as the Volga, in today's Russia. They even reached the city of Constantinople - now Istanbul - the capital of the Byzantine Empire. For the Vikings, these were long and dangerous journeys into the unknown. People the merchants encountered weren't always friendly and a trader carrying valuables was always a target for robbers.

## Selling and buying

Viking merchants carried with them products from Scandinavia, including walrus ivory, amber

16

and furs. They brought back valuable items from the East - gold and silver objects and rare gems - that could be sold for high prices back home.

## Settling new lands

The island of Iceland, in the north Atlantic Ocean, was still uninhabited long after the rest of Europe was settled. Norwegian Viking seafarers discovered the island in the middle CE 800s, and soon shiploads of settlers were heading west, away from crowded living conditions back home. Some Viking explorers travelled even further, founding settlements in Greenland and what is today Newfoundland in Canada.

### IF YOU WERE A VIKING...

To go travelling you would have to be fit, hardy and prepared to leave your family behind, probably forever. You'd need to be able to survive a difficult voyage across rough seas to help set up a lonely settlement in a new land. When you got to your destination you'd need some pretty good survival skills to stay alive!

This reconstructed isolated Viking farming settlement is in Iceland. ▼

# A Viking town

Vikings took over towns in the areas they conquered. In England they made Jorvik - today's York - their capital. Viking kings ruled Jorvik, which grew to be the second-largest city in the country, until 954.

## A bustling capital

Jorvik was repaired and expanded by Vikings. At its height about 10,000 people lived there. They repaired and improved the town's walls, which were originally built by

▲ A reconstructed street scene in busy Jorvik.

the Romans. Many new craft workshops and houses were built and a busy waterfront area handled cargo from all over the Viking world.

## Buying and selling

Before about 1000, Vikings didn't use coins to buy things. They paid for goods with pieces of silver. These could take the form of jewellery, buckles, bars of silver or 'hack-silver' - pieces of larger silver items that had been chopped up. Vikings also bartered (traded one thing for another).

## Craft centre

Jorvik's craft workers included glass-blowers, blacksmiths, sword-makers and leather workers, and jewellers who made stunning brooches from silver, and beads from Baltic amber. Archaeologists have made many important finds at Jorvik. You can see these at the Jorvik Viking Centre in York.

These Viking beads carved out of amber were found at Jorvik.▼

## PRESERVED CLOTHES

Not many items of Viking clothing have survived because fabric and leather rot easily. However, at Jorvik, experts have found Viking shoes and even pieces of cloth. The area of the city in which these items were found is especially boggy and damp and this stopped bacteria from destroying the fragile material.

These Viking shoes were also found at Jorvik. ▼

## Smelly find

Crafted items were not the only things archaeologists found at Jorvik. They also uncovered human poo deposited in the pits Vikings used as toilets. Analysing the poo gave experts clues as to what people living in Jorvik ate.

# Feasting and fun

Vikings loved feasts - big meals where everyone got together - as much as we do today. Vikings liked to have fun too, and sports and games were popular.

## Feasts

Feasts celebrated times of the year like midwinter or a family event, such as a marriage. Viking warriors might hold a feast to celebrate the end of a

▲ Re-enactors dressed as Viking women prepare a feast in a longhouse.

successful raid. Many Vikings lived in isolated communities and transport was difficult, so feasts were a chance for everyone to wear their best clothing and eat and drink long into the night. At a feast there was usually music and entertainment provided by storytellers and musicians.

## Drinking

There was always plenty of drink at a feast, with beer and mead (a drink made from fermented honey) on the menu. These might be served in 'drinking horns', made from the decorated hollowed-out horns of cattle. Drinking from a horn was tricky – get the angle wrong and you could end up wearing your drink as it poured down your front.

## Sports and games

Both Viking adults and children loved sports. Running races, swimming and strength contests, such as throwing a heavy rock over a measured distance, were all popular, as was skating in winter. Skates looked like ordinary Viking shoes with a piece of animal bone attached to the bottom to help the wearer glide on the ice.

**BOARD GAME**

A popular Viking board game was *hnefatafl* (neff-TAH-fell). One player had a king and eight pieces representing soldiers while the other player had sixteen soldier pieces. The player with the king had to move the king from the centre to the edge of the board without being surrounded by the other player's pieces.

# Viking laws

Vikings held regular assemblies to decide important questions. These were called Things, or Althings. A Thing was like a cross between a court of law and a parliament.

## THE TYNWALD

On the Isle of Man, which was settled by Norwegian Vikings, there was a Thing called the Tynwald. Laws were read out, debated and agreed by those present. The Tynwald still exists today and is one of the oldest parliaments in the world. Every year, usually on 5 July, the Tynwald meets outside on Tynwald Hill, the site of the old Viking parliament.

## Having your say

There were both small local Things and larger regional meetings. Here Vikings made new laws and explained existing laws to people who had gathered. Every free Viking, including women, had the right to speak.

Tynwald Hill on the Isle of Man has four circular platforms. The centre platform is 3.7 m high. ▼

The Thing also passed judgement on people who had broken laws and decided which punishments to impose. These could be extreme and included death or maiming (the chopping off of body parts).

## Feuds

Vikings could be quarrelsome and slights against a family's honour were felt deeply. As a result one Viking family often had a long-running dispute with another. These feuds could last for generations, especially if a murder was involved. One of the ways a Thing could try to end a feud was by ordering the payment of 'blood money' to avenge a death.

Vikings came from far and wide to attend a Thing. It was an important social occasion. ▼

## Social gatherings

Vikings often lived far from each other. Attending a Thing was a good chance to meet other Vikings, catch up on the latest news and, for unmarried people, perhaps to find a wife or husband.

## Getting to the Thing

Travel in Viking lands could be a challenge and roads, where they existed at all, were very poor. Vikings preferred to travel by boat, but if this wasn't an option people rode on horseback, travelled in horse-drawn carts if they were wealthy, or walked. Winter journeys could be made on sledges or skis.

# Gods and religion

Early Vikings were pagan, meaning they worshipped a number of gods and goddesses. Over time, however, Vikings converted to Christianity.

## Important gods

Vikings traditionally believed in several gods, who lived in a magical place called Asgard. Odin was the chief god, deciding who won or lost battles. He had

▲ This Viking gravestone dating from the 700s shows Odin (at the top) riding his eight-legged horse, Sleipnir.

three wives: Fjorgyn, Frigga and Rind. Thor was the sky god, who controlled storms and the weather. The goddess Freya was in charge of love and beauty, while Idun was the goddess of spring and youth.

## Viking worship

Vikings had few temples or places of worship. The main feature of Viking worship was a ritual meal or feast called a *blót* (blessing). Here, animals such as pigs and horses were sacrificed and eaten. There were blót in autumn, at midwinter and in the spring.

## Burial customs

When a Viking chieftain died it was the custom to bury him in his ship so he could sail into the afterlife. Dressed in his best clothing, he was entombed with valuable possessions, such as his sword. Animals, including horses

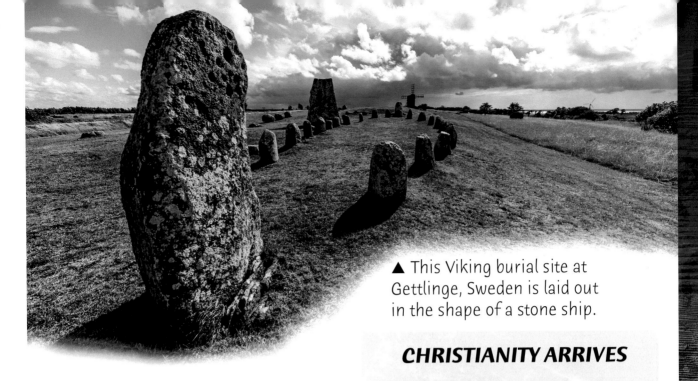

▲ This Viking burial site at Gettlinge, Sweden is laid out in the shape of a stone ship.

and hunting dogs were killed and buried with him, too. In some cases the ship wasn't buried but set on fire to send him quickly to the afterlife. This tradition is re-enacted at the Shetland festival of Up Helly Aa (see page 27) today.

## CHRISTIANITY ARRIVES

Christianity took longer to arrive in the Viking homelands than in other lands, partly due to their remoteness. In the 960s King Harald Bluetooth of Denmark became Christian, followed in the 1020s by King Olaf Haraldsson of Norway.

## THOR'S HAMMER

Thor, the son of Odin and Fjorgyn, was armed with a powerful magical hammer called Mjöllnir. With this he protected Asgard and righted wrongs. Many Vikings wore a hammer pendant, believing it protected them, too.

# Art, culture and stories

Vikings had their own distinct alphabet and style of art. Many Viking stories were written down long after the Viking Age so we can read them today.

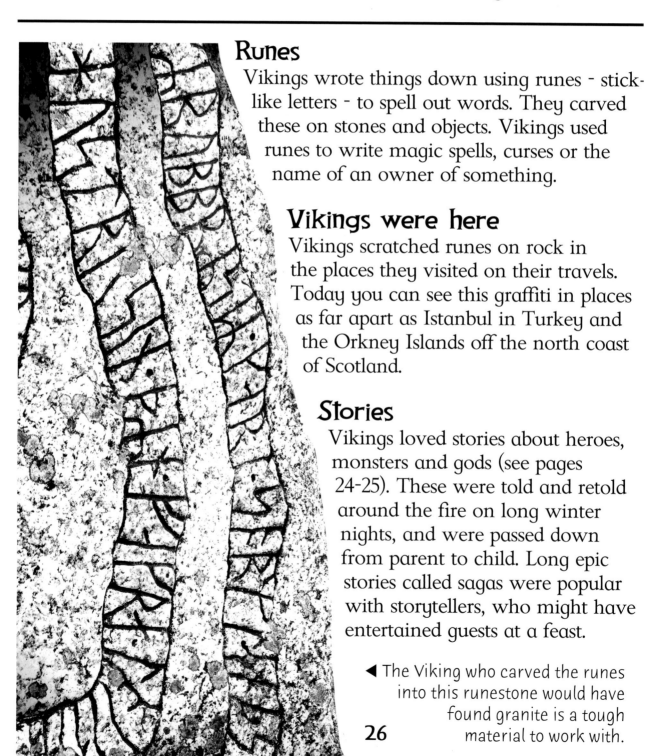

## Runes

Vikings wrote things down using runes - stick-like letters - to spell out words. They carved these on stones and objects. Vikings used runes to write magic spells, curses or the name of an owner of something.

## Vikings were here

Vikings scratched runes on rock in the places they visited on their travels. Today you can see this graffiti in places as far apart as Istanbul in Turkey and the Orkney Islands off the north coast of Scotland.

## Stories

Vikings loved stories about heroes, monsters and gods (see pages 24-25). These were told and retold around the fire on long winter nights, and were passed down from parent to child. Long epic stories called sagas were popular with storytellers, who might have entertained guests at a feast.

◄ The Viking who carved the runes into this runestone would have found granite is a tough material to work with.

## NJÁLS SAGA

This famous saga describes a long-running feud between two Icelandic Viking families in the years between 960 and 1020. It was first written down around 1300. Rather like gang warfare today, members of each family, thinking they have been insulted, defend their honour by taking bloody revenge on members of the other. Magic, fate, omens and dreams all figure in this violent tale.

## Up Helly Aa

The Up Helly Aa winter festival in Lerwick in the Shetland Islands celebrates Viking culture. Held every year on the last Tuesday in January, islanders and visitors dress as Vikings and march through the streets of the town with torches, singing Viking songs. At the height of the celebrations a replica Viking longship is set on fire. See page 25.

◀ At the height of the Up Helly Aa celebrations a replica Viking longship is set on fire.

# What happened to the Vikings?

**The Vikings were one of the most feared and fascinating peoples in history. So what happened to them?**

## Intermarriage

Many Vikings married people already living in places where they settled. The children of these marriages had both Viking and native blood, so the Viking bloodline changed over time. But even today there are many who can claim to be at least part Viking. A recent study of British DNA suggested that more than one million people have Viking ancestors. Nearly 30 per cent of people living in Shetland are direct descendants of Vikings.

## Vikings rule England

In 1015 a huge Viking army attacked England. Led by Danish prince Cnut, forces besieged London and eventually forced Edmund, the Anglo-Saxon king, to divide his kingdom. The northern part went to the Vikings and the southern part was to remain Anglo-Saxon until Edmund's death. Edmund died just a few weeks after the agreement so Cnut became king of England. He reigned for 19 years until Anglo-Saxons briefly regained the throne.

This medieval manuscript shows Edmund and Cnut fighting at the Battle of Assandun, England. ▼

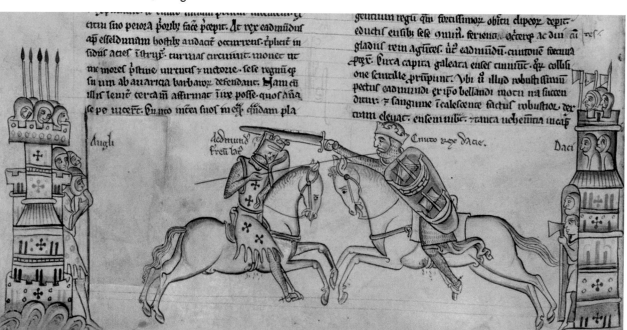

▲ King Rollo's tomb is located in Rouen Cathedral, which is in northern France. Rollo – a Viking and the first ruler of Normandy – converted to Christianity.

# Normans

Vikings who settled in Normandy became Christian and learned to speak French. In 1066 Duke William of Normandy, a descendant of the Viking chieftain Rollo, defeated the Anglo-Saxons at the Battle of Hastings and became the first Norman king of England.

▲ A silver coin showing King Cnut.

### OTHER LANDS

In other places – such as Iceland – where Vikings settled, people retained their Viking culture, laws and traditions, only changing these gradually over time. This is evident in these places today. People are proud to have Viking ancestors.

29

# Glossary

**Amber** Ancient hardened sap from trees used as a gemstone.

**Analyse** To examine evidence.

**Anglo-Saxons** The people who lived in England at the time Vikings began to raid.

**Archaeologist** An expert who unearths objects from the past and works out their meaning.

**Bloodthirsty** Violent.

**Boggy** Earth that is spongy and wet.

**Bow** The front of a boat or ship.

**Byzantine Empire** An empire in the eastern Mediterranean area that existed from CE 330 to 1453.

**Chain mail** Interlocking rings that protected the wearer from sword or axe cuts.

**Chieftain** A local leader or warlord.

**Christian** Someone who believes that Jesus Christ was the son of God.

**Cloak** A large heavy garment worn over the shoulders to keep warm.

**Convert** To change religion.

**Epic** Long, difficult or amazing.

**Fate** The spiritual power that some people believe determines what happens in a person's life.

**Feud** A long-standing row between families or peoples.

**Hearth** The place in a home where a fire is burned.

**Hose** Long thick woollen stockings.

**Hull** The main body of a boat or ship.

**Isolated** Far apart, lonely.

**Jarl** A Viking lord.

**Karl** A free Viking.

**Keel** The 'backbone' of a wooden ship.

**Omen** A magical sign that warns of an upcoming event, usually bad.

**Pagan** Believing in many gods and goddesses.

**Parliament** A gathering where laws are made.

**Pickle** To preserve food in salty water to keep it from going off.

**Runes** The Viking alphabet.

**Scandinavia** In the Viking age, the region of northern Europe that is now Denmark, Norway and Sweden.

**Settler** Someone who goes to make a new life in an uninhabited land.

**Thrall** A Viking slave.

**Tunic** A long shirt reaching to the knees.

**Uninhabited** A place where no people live.

**Walrus ivory** A hard white precious substance from the tusks of walruses and used to make jewellery and other items.

# Some Viking websites

www.bbc.co.uk/education/topics/ztyr9j6
The BBCs primary history section on Vikings and Viking life.

www.jorvik-viking-centre-co.uk
Explore this important Viking site and visitor attraction in York.

www.museumoflondon.co.uk
The Museum of London records the history of London and its collections include Vikings artefacts found in the River Thames.

Note to parents and teachers: Every effort has been made by the Publishers to ensure that the websites in this book are suitable for children, that they are of the highest educational value, and that they contain no inappropriate or offensive material. However, because of the nature of the Internet, it is impossible to guarantee that the contents of these sites will not be altered. We strongly advise that Internet access is supervised by a responsible adult.

# Timeline

CE 793  First Viking raid at Lindisfarne on the north-east coast of England

799  First Viking raids on France

800  Vikings land in Orkney, Shetland and the Faroe Islands

810  Vikings raid present-day Netherlands and northern Germany

860  Vikings trade in Russia and reach Constantinople in Turkey

866  Viking army invades England, looking for land to settle

867  Vikings capture York and rebuild it as Jorvik

870  Vikings discover Iceland and begin to settle there

878  Anglo-Saxon King Alfred the Great of Wessex defeats Viking leader Guthrum at the Battle of Edington

911  Vikings begin to settle in Normandy

960  King Harald Bluetooth of Denmark converts to Christianity

982  Vikings discover Greenland

986  Vikings discover North America

995  King Olaf of Norway converts to Christianity

1001  Vikings founded a short-lived colony in Newfoundland

1066  Norman Duke William is victorious over Anglo-Saxon forces at the Battle of Hastings. William becomes king of England

1100  End of the Viking Age

# Index